Dear Triune God,
I want to seek You
and find You in all things, and be with You,
listen to You, and get in sync with Your heartbeat.
Jesus in me, Holy Spirit in me,
let me live with Your reality very near,
filling my spirit.
Amen.

Introduction

Since the beginning of time, Triune God has been active in the earth. In the beginning the Spirit hovered over the void, God spoke the creative word and all creation appeared, and Jesus was there. (Proverbs 8:22-31) Each one brings His own Person to the relationship. They have been entirely complete in each other since eternity past in total perfection and unity.

Luke provided one Trinity mention with the annunciation to Mary about the birth and mission of Jesus. All three persons of God were involved. The angel said, *"The Holy Spirit will come upon you, and the power of the Most High will overshadow you. So, the holy one to be born will be called the Son of God"* (Luke 1:35). There is Father, Son, and Holy Spirit in one verse.

At His baptism, Jesus saw the Spirit of God descending like a dove and lighting on Him. A voice from heaven said, *"This is my Son, whom I love; with Him I am well pleased"* (Matthew 3:16-17).

One of the last earthly statements of Jesus mentions all three members of the Trinity. He said to the disciples, *"… Go and make disciples of all nations, baptizing them in the name of the Father and of the Son and of the Holy Spirit…"* (Matthew 28:19).

Trinity prayer is found in the Epistles. In 2 Corinthians 16:14 Paul blessed the Corinthians. *"May the grace of the Lord Jesus Christ, and the love of God, and the fellowship of the Holy Spirit be with you all."* Paul requested prayer in Romans 15:30 mentioning the Trinity. *"I urge you, brothers, by our Lord Jesus Christ and by the love of the Spirit, to join me in my struggle by praying to God for me"* (Romans 15:30). The Message puts it this way. *"We have one request,*

dear friends: Pray for us. Pray strenuously with and for us—
to God the Father, through the power of our Master Jesus,
through the love of the Spirit" (Romans 15:30).

Peter addressed His first epistle to God's people, chosen according to the foreknowledge of God the Father, through the sanctifying work of the Holy Spirit, for obedience to Jesus and sprinkling by His blood (1 Peter 1:2). So, the Trinity pattern was known to the early church and established before the New Testament was written.

In Trinity praying I feel completeness in talking to God in His completeness. It is a great theological and experiential challenge to enter into this deep conversational communion with the Trinity. I treasure the glory of their separate Persons and offices. I know that to seek anything from One is to seek the response of all of God, because He is inseparable.

How well do you know God the Father, God the Son, and God the Holy Spirit? Although we say we believe in the Trinity, we probably tend to pray to one Person of the Trinity. We may ask God about big stuff—wars, environmental catastrophe, starving people in Africa. When we speak of prayer as conversation, we may mean with Jesus our Friend who is involved in daily matters, like "Help me make it through today." Most think of the Holy Spirit as a symbol, a power, or an experience but not a Person.

This is an invitation to move past supplication into declaration of all of God as a way of life. We could never get to the end of praising the Father, the Son, and the Holy Spirit for who He is, in this life or in eternity, if we knew all there is to know about Him. Is this all the Trinity prayers and declarations that could be written? By no means! These eternal truths can be savored time and time again. I want this to move you to intimacy with Father, Son, and Holy Spirit. I pray that His breath will infuse His Word and make it come alive.

Trinity Prayers

Delighting In His Majesty And Supremacy

Read these declarations of truth about the majesty and supremacy of God, but don't just read them. Take these truths in. They are for intimacy, not just information. Selah. Pause. Don't be so jaded by familiarity that you miss these heart-stopping revelations of God.

Let all three Persons of His being plant this deep within in awe and reverence and wonder. Ask Him to show you how to take in the sublime revelation of who He is and then respond from a full and overflowing heart. Let your spirit receive this from God. Don't move on to the next triplet until each one is deep within you. Respond to Him.

I am lifting my heart to…
The Three of Intimacy
The Three of Redemption
The Three of Power

Exclaim with all the angels, "How great you are!"

He is able.

I am praising that...
The Father is able to do all things, exceedingly beyond all asking.
Eph 3:20, 2 Cor 9:8, Phil 3:21, 2 Tim 1:12
The Son entered into heaven itself, now to appear in the presence of God for us. Heb 9:24
The Spirit bears witness to Jesus living in us. 1 John 3:24

Praise Him. Say to Him, "You are awesome!"

He is acquainted with all our ways.

I am persuaded that...
The Father is the keeper of our times. Ps 31:15
The Son knows us and calls us by name. John 10:14, 3
The Spirit empowers proclamation.
Rom 15:18-19, 1 Cor 2:4, 1 Peter 1:12

Be confident that He knows you intimately.

He has all-authority.

I fall down before Him.
The Father is ruler over nations, ruler of all things.
Ps 22:28, 1 Chron 29:12
The Son is the head of the church, the head of every man who invites us to grow up into all things in him. Eph 4:15, Col 1:18, 1 Cor 11:3
The Spirit of God empowered Jesus with authority to drive out demons.
Matt 12:28

Bow in silent awe of His authority and rule.

He is the beginning and end.

I lift my hands to...
The Father who is the God of knowledge, who knows the end from the beginning. 1 Sam 2:3, Isa 46:10
The Son who is the beginning and the end. Rev 22:13
The Spirit whom God promised forever and who is part of the covenant with us and our children and their descendants. Isa 59:21

Be still and know that He is God.

He is the bread.

I am nourished by…
The Father who gave the manna in the wilderness. Deut 8:16, Ps 78:24
The Son who is the Bread of life, living bread from heaven. John 6:23, 51
The Spirit who fills afresh with Himself as His people pray. Acts 4:31
Pause and let Him feed you the Word of Life.

The Christmas story is his-story.

I adore him because…
The Father sent wise men from afar, guided by a star in the east and
bringing expensive gifts of worship— gold, frankincense, and myrrh.
Matt 2:2, 11
The Son is the Star out of Jacob. Num 24:1
The Spirit alone can restrain lawlessness and provide "Glory to God in
the highest, and on earth peace, goodwill toward men."
2 Thes 2:7, Luke 2:14 NKJV
O come, let us adore Him!

He is a consuming fire.

I stand amazed that…
The Father is a consuming fire. Heb 12:29
The Son was nailed to the cross, crucified for sin. Acts 2:23,36
The Spirit gave the prophets power to denounce sin. Micah 3:8
Exalt Him that His holiness was satisfied in the death of Jesus for you.

He is the counselor.

I give thanks that…
The Father counsels us with His eye upon us and sent us the
Counselor, the Holy Spirit, in Jesus' name. Ps 32:8, John 14:26
The Son is Wonderful Counselor. Isa 9:6
The Spirit is the Counselor given by the Father and the Son.
John 14:16, 26; 15:26, 16:7
Commit your way to Him.

He is covenant-keeping God.

I praise Him that...
The Father is Abraham's God. Gen 26:24, Exo 3:6
Jesus is the seed of Abraham. Matt 1:1, Gal 3:16
The Holy Spirit is the Spirit of promise. Eph 1:13

Selah... pause and take this in.

He is Creator.

I worship Him that...
The Father created the heaven and the earth and everything in it.
Gen 1:1-2:1
Through the Son all things were made. John 1:2-3, 1 Cor 8:6,
Col 1:16, Heb 1:2
The Spirit existed in tri-unity before time and participated with
God in the creation of the world. Gen 1:1-2, Ps 104:30

Join all creation in declaring His glory.

He is God of desert places.

I am grateful that...
The Father led His people as His sheep in the desert.
Ps 78:52, Isa 48:21
The Son defeated the tempter in the desert. Matt 4:1,
Luke 4:1, 14
The Spirit was the fullness of power for the desert.
Luke 4:1, 14

Ponder His power in your life.

He is deliverance and help.

He has done this...
The Father sent a deliverer. Judges 3:15
The Son was the deliverer sent by the Father. Rom 11:26
The Spirit gives help when we cry. Phil 1:19

Bless the Lord, O my soul.

He draws all men to Himself.

I am humbled that...
The Father draws men to Jesus by cords of everlasting love
and human kindness. John 6:44, Jer 31:3, Hos 11:4
The Son, being lifted up, draws all men to Himself. John 12:32
The Spirit testifies concerning Jesus. John 15:26

Amen. Thank Him.

He is El Shaddai.

I stand in awe that...
The Father is El Shaddai, all-sufficient one. Gen 17:1
The Son is exalted to the highest place and before him every knee will
bow. Phil 2:9-11
The Holy Spirit reveals the mystery of Christ. Eph 3:5

All that is within me, bless His holy name.

He is eternal.

He is past, present, and future.
The Father is from everlasting to everlasting, without beginning or end,
everlasting Father, everlasting light. Ps 90:2 Isa 9:6, Isa 60:20
The Son is the resurrection and the life, risen Lord.
John 11:25, Luke 24:34
The Spirit is the seven-fold Spirit of the Lord. Isa 11:2, Rev 1:4

Selah... pause and soak this in.

He is eternal.

I am in awe that...
The Father is the one from whom and through whom
and to whom are all things. Rom 11:36
Jesus the Son was before all things. Col 1:17
The Spirit tells us what is to come. John 16:13

Stand in awe of Him.

He is exalted.

I fall on my face that…
The Father is exalted God, exalted in power, exalted over all the nations, His glory above the heavens. Micah 6:6, Job 36:22, Ps 113:4
The Son is exalted above the heavens, to the right hand of God. Heb 7:26, Acts 2:33
The Spirit transported Elijah, Ezekiel, Philip, and John. 1 Kings 18:12; Eze 3:12, 14; 8:3; 11:1,24; 37:1, 43:5; Acts 8:39, Rev 17:3, 21:10

Exalt Him in your life.

He is faith.

I bow my knees that…
The Father loved the world so much that He sent His only Son so that whoever trusts Him might have eternal life. John 3:16, John 17:2
The Son is the author and finisher of faith. Heb 12:2
The Spirit purifies our hearts by faith. Acts 15:9

Let your heart resonate with Him in faith.

God's family begins with Him.

He gives us a new bloodline.
The Father is our Abba and calls us His child. Rom 8:14-16
The Son is our brother. John 20:17, Heb 2:11
The Spirit is the Spirit of sonship by whom we cry "Abba, Father." Rom 8:15

Respond to His love with love from your whole heart.

He forgives.

Let the redeemed of the Lord say this:
The Father is longsuffering, forgiving iniquity and transgression. Num 14:18 NKJV (forgiving sin and rebellion, NIV)
The Son is the sin-bearing sacrifice. Rom 3:25
The Spirit washed away our sins, set us apart for God, made us right with Him. 1 Cor 6:11 NLT

Bow your heart before Him.

He Is the Gardener, Vine, and Fruit

He is life-giving, and I thrive in His hands.
The Father is the gardener, the vinedresser. John 15:1
The Son is the Vine, we are His branches. John 15:5
The Spirit is the fruit of the Spirit in us. Gal 5:22-23, 25
Be intentional to stay connected to Him.

He Is God of Glory

I give Him the reverence due Him.
The Father is majestic in holiness, awesome in glory,
doing wonders. Exo 15:11
The Son is the radiance of God's glory. Heb 1:3
The Spirit shows the glory in the throneroom. Rev 1:10, 4:2
Let all the earth keep silence before Him.

He Is God of Glory
I declare that...

The Father raised us up with Christ and seated us with Him in the
heavenly realms. Eph 2:6
The Son is the light for revelation and for glory. Luke 2:32
The Spirit transforms us from glory to glory. 2 Cor 3:18
Give witness to His glory.

He is God of my praise.

His presence inspires me to praise and obedience.
The Father is God of our praise. Ps 109:1
The Son is the same, yesterday and today and forever.
Heb 13:8
The Spirit inspires obedience. Eze 36:27
Spread out your hands to Him.

He is God of the impossible.

I exercise my faith that…
The Father is the Sovereign Lord, God of all impossibilities.
Jer 32:17, 26; Isa 28:16
The Son said, "With God all things are possible." Matt 19:26
The Spirit gives all the gifts of wisdom, knowledge, faith, healing,
miracles, prophecy, discernment, tongues, and
interpretations. 1 Cor 12:4,7-10

Praise Him, for He is worthy.

He is God who sees.

I am confident because…
The Father is God who sees (Elroi). Gen 16:13
The Son does what He sees His Father doing and says what
His Father is saying. John 5:19-20, 8:26
The Spirit gives us God's wise counsel. 1 Cor 7:40

Praise Him that He is all-seeing.

He is goodness.

I rest in Him because…
The Father stores up His goodness for us. Ps 31:19-21
The Son is the Good Shepherd. John 10:11
The good Spirit leads and instructs us. Ps 143:10, Neh 9:20

Lean into His goodness.

He is healer.

I exalt His healing name.
The Father is Jehovah-Rapha, the Lord who heals.
Exo 15:26
The Son heals every kind of sickness. Matt 4:23-24, 8:13,
16; 9:35, 12:15, 14:14, 15:30
The Spirit gives gifts of healing. 1 Cor 12:9

How pleasant and fitting it is to praise Him for health and healing!

He is holiness.

I am awestruck that…
The Father is the Holy One of Israel. Isa 41:16
The Son is the Holy One of God, who reconciled us to the Father by His physical body through death to present us holy in his sight, without blemish and free from accusation.
John 6:69, 2 Cor 5:18-19, Col 1:22
The Holy Spirit is the eternal Spirit through whom Jesus offered Himself without spot to God. Heb 9:14 NKJV

Walk in the light of His holiness.

He is holy.

It is infinitely amazing that…
The holy Father forgives iniquities. Micah 7:18
The blood of the holy Son purifies us from sin. 1 John 1:7, Titus 2:14
The Spirit of holiness declared Jesus to be the Son in power.
Rom 1:4 ESV

Pause and take this in.

He is I am.

He is supreme over all.
The Father is the I AM that I AM. Exo 3:14
The Son is ascended to the right hand of the Father.
Eph 4:10, Heb 12:2
The Spirit searches the deep things of God. 1 Cor 2:10

Open your mouth wide and He will fill it.

He is incarnate.

I marvel that…
The Father walked the earth in the person of Jesus and is Jesus in me. John 1:14, 17:23
The Son was incarnate, the Man Christ Jesus, the Man whom God appointed. 1 Tim 2:5, Acts 17:31
The Spirit lives in me. Rom 8:11, Eph 2:22, 1 Cor 3:16

Tell God what this means to you.

He is the Judge.

I rise to acknowledge the Judge.
The Father is the judicial Ancient of Days. Dan 7:9, 22
The Son judges all things, the living and the dead. John 5:22,
2 Tim 4:1
The Spirit guards the good deposit entrusted to me. 2 Tim 1:14

"Yes, your honor."

He is Judge of all the earth.

Mercy is my only plea.
The Father is the Judge of all the earth. Gen 18:25
The Son is my advocate. 1 John 2:1 NKJV, Heb 9:24
In the Spirit there is freedom. 2 Cor 3:18

"Yes, your honor."

He is God of Justice.

I tremble that...
The Father is Jehovah-Mishpat, the God of justice. Isa 30:18
The Son has all authority to judge as the Son of Man, whose
judgment is just and right and true. John 5:22, 27, 30; 8:16
The Spirit is the spirit of justice. Isa 28:6

"Yes, your honor."

He is the beginning and end of justice.

Thank you...
Father, for being our Lawgiver, Judge, and King. Isa 33:22,
James 4:12
Jesus, for cancelling the written code, with its regulations, that
was against us and that stood opposed to us, taking it away,
nailing it to the cross. Col 2:14
Holy Spirit, for standing opposite the law. Gal 5:18

"Yes, your honor."

He is the King.

I have an audience with the King.
The Father is Lord God Almighty and King of the ages,
enthroned as King forever. Rev 15:3, Ps 29:10
The Son is Lord of glory, King of kings and Lord of lords.
1 Cor 2:8, Rev 19:16
The Spirit witnesses that Jesus is exalted to God's own right
hand as Prince and Savior. Acts 5:31-32

Bow before the King.

He is King of Glory.

I am overcome with wonder that…
The Father is the King of glory. Ps 24:10
The Son is Christ in us, the hope of glory. Col 1:27
The Spirit is the Spirit of glory and of God on us. 1 Peter 4:14

Bow your heart before His glory.

He knows our name.

He knows us as family.
The Father determines the number of stars and calls them
each by name. Ps 147:4
The Son is the Son of David, the son of Abraham. Matt 1:1
The Spirit of adoption bears witness with our spirit that we are
children of God. Rom 8:15-16 NKJV

Ask Him what name He calls you.

He is life.

I take refuge in…
The Father who is the Living God in whose hand is our
life and breath. 1 Tim 4:10, Job 12:10
The Son who is the way, the truth, and the life. John 14:6
The Spirit, the Helper, who abides with us forever.
John 14:16 NKJV

Prepare the way for Him.

He has the power of life and death.

I have hope because…
The Father swallowed up death. 1 Cor 15:54
The Son destroyed the power of death and gives us victory.
Heb 2:14, 1 Cor 15:54,57
The Holy Spirit is the Spirit of life in Christ Jesus. Rom 8:2

Praise Him.

He is light and truth.

I walk in the light because…
The Father of lights does not change. James 1:17
Jesus the Son is true light, who gives light to every man. John 1:9
The Holy Spirit knows all things and teaches all things
and is all truth. John 14:26

Fix your eyes on Him.

He is God of Light.

I will not be shaken because…
The Father is God of light, who lives in unapproachable light.
1 John 1:5, 1 Tim 6:16
The Son gives entrance into the kingdom of light. Col 1:13-14
The Spirit reveals the things of God given to me, the things
that He has prepared. 1 Cor 2:10-12

Express your confidence in Him.

He is limitless.

I can never strain His supply because…
The Father is the God of the impossible. Luke 1:37,
Jer 32:27
The Son has all authority and gives us authority. Matt 28:18,
Luke 10:19-20
The Spirit is given by God without limit. John 3:34

Praise Him that He is without limit.

He is the Living God.

He is alive!
The Father is the living God, my rock, my fortress, my deliverer, my refuge, my shield, the horn of my salvation, my stronghold, worthy of praise and I am saved from my enemies. 1 Tim 4:10, Ps 18:1-3
The Son of the living God is the exact representation of His being. Matt 16:16-17, Heb 1:3
The Spirit of the living God writes on the hearts of men. 2 Cor 3:3
Delight in Him.

He is Lord.

He is enthroned on my praise.
The Father is God of gods and Lord of lords, the great God, mighty and awesome. Deut 10:17
The Son is Lord to the glory of God the Father. Phil 2:11
By the Spirit I say "Jesus is Lord." 1 Cor 12:3
Bow before Him.

His ownership compels me.

He is due my willing and complete obedience.
The Father is Adonai, Lord and master, Lord of all. Ps 68:19, Rom 10:12
The Son is the Word of life. 1 John 1:1
The Spirit speaks words of warning. Heb 3:7
Submit to Him.

He is Lord of the whole earth.

I praise You...
Father, You are Lord of heaven and earth. Matt 11:25
I praise You, Jesus, You are most exalted of the kings of the earth. Ps 89:27
I praise You, Spirit, You are the power and witness of God to the ends of the earth. Acts 1:8
Praise Him for His rule to the ends of the earth.

He is Maker of heaven and earth.

He is the first cause of everything.
The Father is the Maker of heaven and earth, from whom our help comes. Ps 121:2
The Son upholds all things by His powerful word. Heb 1:3
The Spirit, the Breath of the Almighty, who made us, breathes His breath into us, and sustains our life. Job 33:4, John 20:22

Thank Him for His sustaining care.

He makes all things new.

He makes my heart glad.
The Father is making all things new. Isa 42:6
Jesus makes all things new. Rev 21:5
The Spirit renews the face of the earth. Ps 104:30

Set your hope on Him.

He is mercy.

His tenderness melts my heart.
The Father crowns us with tender mercies. Ps 103:4 KJV, Eph 2:4-5
The Son is the high priest of all mercy. Heb 2:17
The Spirit of grace is the mediator of all grace. Zech 12:10, Heb 10:29

From His heart receive His tender grace.

He is Mighty God.

My heart trusts Him because…
The Father is the Mighty God, mighty warrior who fights on our behalf. Isa 9:6, Isa 42:13, Jer 20:11
The Son keeps the keys of Hades and death. Rev 1:18
The Spirit vindicates the life and work of Jesus. 1 Tim 3:16

Give Him the glory due His name.

He defined the mission of Jesus.

He is on mission in the earth.
The Father will not break a bruised reed nor snuff out a smoldering wick.
Isa 42:3
The Son preaches good news to the poor, binds up the broken-hearted,
proclaims freedom for prisoners, gives sight to the blind, releases the
bruised and oppressed. Luke 4:18-19
The Spirit defined the mission of the Son and anoints Him to do all these
things. Luke 4:18

Receive this gladly.

He is the Name.

I exalt You…
Father, El Elyon God most high, the everlasting name.
Ps 83:18, Mark 5:7, Isa 63:13
I exalt You, Jesus, name above all names. Phil 2:9
I exalt You, Spirit, in whose name we were baptized, giving
us authority in the Spirit of God and the Spirit of Christ Jesus.
Matt 28:19, Rom 8:9

Gaze upon His beauty.

There is no other God.

There is none like him.
The Father is holy, eternal, immortal, invisible, the only God, and to Him
is due honor and glory forever. 1 Peter 1:16, 1 Tim 1:17
The Son is the Lamb of God slain from the creation of the world, who
takes away the sin of the world, who died and rose and lives again.
Rev 13:8, John 1:29, Rom 14:9
The Spirit was active in God's mercy in saving us, through the washing of
regeneration and renewing of the Holy Spirit, whom He poured out on
us abundantly through Jesus Christ our Savior. Titus 3:5-6

Soak in His magnificence.

There is none-other like our God.

He is without equal.
The Father is the Lord God; there is no other besides Him. He is Majesty in heaven. Deut 4:35, Exo 15:11, Heb 1:3
The Son sings over us as the Morning Star among the morning stars; thus, He leads angel choirs to sing over us. Job 38:7
Through the Spirit it is not us speaking but Him who will give us what to say at the right time. Mark 13:11

Sing a new song to Him.

He is over all.

I set my heart's affection on Him and give Him my life's devotion.
The Father is the one God and Father of all, who is over all
and through all and in all. Eph 4:5
The Son is the Amen, the faithful and true witness. Rev 3:14
The Spirit works unity, baptizing us into one body. 1 Cor 12:4,11,13;
Eph 4:3-4

Triune God, be lifted up in my life.

He has all power.

I am dwarfed by His power.
The Father is all-powerful. Rev 19:6 KJV
The Son is the power of God and the wisdom of God. 1 Cor 1:24
The Spirit comes upon us in power. Acts 1:8

Be blessed in the revelation of his infinite power.

He is all-powerful.

I acknowledge his might.
The Father sent His glorious arm of power to divide the waters before His people. Isa 63:12
The Son destroyed death and brought life and immortality to light. 2 Tim 1:10
The Spirit is the power by whom Jesus taught, healed, did mighty miracles and preached the gospel on earth. Luke 4:14

Be blessed in His sovereign rule.

He initiates prayer.

I delight to call upon Him.
The Father honors prayers in Jesus' name. John 14:13-14
The Son through whom we pray is ever interceding for us.
John 16:26, Heb 7:25
The Holy Spirit intercedes according to the will of the Father.
Rom 8:27

Thank Him for His ministry of intercession.

He is Redeemer.

My life is based on His redemption.
The Father is Redeemer and we know that our Redeemer
lives. Job 19:25, Isa 42:6, Jer 50:34
The Son is our spiritual Rock. 1 Cor 10:4
The Spirit of sonship banishes slavery to fear. Rom 8:15

Let the redeemed of the Lord say so.

He is Root, Branch, and Fruit.

He is the root of righteousness.
The Father pulls up by the root everything that He has not planted.
Matt 15:13
The Son is the Root of David and the righteous Branch.
Rev 5:5, Jer 23:5
The Spirit gives the first fruits of the Spirit, a foretaste of living
in God's presence forever. Rom 8:23

Receive His gift of righteousness.

He is salvation.

I will make Him known through all generations.
The Father is mighty to save, who did not spare His own Son
but gave Him up for us. Zeph 3:17, Rom 8:32
The Son is Christ the Messiah. John 20:31, John 1:41
The Spirit gives birth to spirit. John 3:6

Speak of His great salvation that is full and free.

He is sanctification.

I thank Him for His cleansing power.
The Father is good and His love endures forever. Ps 107:1
The Son washes, sanctifies, and justifies for His name's sake. 1 Cor 6:11
The Spirit is the Spirit of judgment and fire. Isa 4:4

All that is within you, bless His holy name.

He sets captives free.

The Triune God came to heal the broken-hearted and set
the captives free…
In the love of the Father. Ps 147:3, 103:4
In the ministry of Jesus. Luke 4:18-19
In the power of the Holy Spirit. Isa 61:1-3

Freely worship Him in spirit and in truth for comfort and freedom.

He is the Son.

I love His revelation of Himself.
The Father spoke to us by His Son. Heb 1:2
Jesus is the One and Only Son, the Child Jesus, Firstborn Son, Firstborn
of creation, the Obedient Son. John 1:14, Luke 2:27, Ps 89:27, Col 1:15,
Heb 5:8-9
The Spirit conceived the Son in His mother's womb on this earth.
Matt 1:18,20; Luke 1:35

Hear Him today.

He is sovereign.

I bow my will before…
The Father whose plans cannot be thwarted. Job 42:2, Isa 14:27
The Son who is God over all. Rom 9:5
The Spirit who controls my mind with life and peace. Rom 8:6

Submit to Him.

He spoke.

I open my heart to Him.
The Father spoke worlds into being and spoke to us by His Son.
Gen 1, Heb 1:2
The Son is the Chosen One of God, God's Christ, and by Him, and for
Him, and in Him are all things. Luke 23:35, 1 Peter 2:4, Col 1:16-17
The Spirit spoke through Moses, David, Isaiah, Ezekiel, the
prophets, and John. Num 11:25, 2 Sam 23:2, Matt 22:43,
Mark 12:36, Acts 4:25; Acts 28:2, Eze 11:5, 2 Peter 1:21, Rev 14:13

Pause in complete wonderment.

He is supreme.

I speak of His excellence.
The Father is infinite, and His understanding has no limit. Ps 147:5
The Son has the supremacy in all things through the fullness of God.
Col 1:18-19
The Spirit has a glorious ministry. 2 Cor 3:8

Bow before His power in the world and in your life.

He is revealed in symbols.

I am satisfied in Him.
The Father was seen in cloud and fire. Exo 13:21
The Son is the door and the shepherd of the sheep.
John 10:7, 9, 11, 14
The Holy Spirit is pictured as a dove, flame, and living water.
Matt 3:16, Acts 2:3-4, John 7:37-39

Tell Him that He is all in all to you.

He is Teacher.

He is personal to me.
The Father is our instructor. Ps 32:8
The Son is the Teacher from God. John 3:2
The Spirit gives the counsel of God. 1 Cor 7:40

Thank Him that you are the apple of His eye.

He is Truth.

His truth abides in me.
The Father gives anointing to know the truth. 1 John 2:20, 27
The Son gives us His mind. 1 Cor 2:16
The Spirit brings to remembrance Christ's words that He has said.
John 14:26
Welcome the One who is true.

His truth abides in us.

I love His plumbline of three-fold truth.
The Father is God of truth. Ps 31:5
The Son is the way, the truth, and the life. John 14:6
The Spirit is the Spirit of truth. John 14:16-1
Let this sink deeply into your inmost being and choose to line up with it.

He is the God of victory.

I take confidence that…
The Father is Lord of hosts, God of angel armies.
Ps 24:10 NKJV
The Son disarmed all principalities and authorities, triumphing
over them by his cross. Col 2:15
The Spirit is the sword of spiritual warfare. Eph 6:17
Shout, "Hallelujah!"

He is the God of warfare.

I thank Him that He gives victories.
The Father is the shadow of the Almighty. Ps 91:1
The Son overcame the adversary by His blood. Rev 12:11
The Spirit is the presence of God everywhere. Ps 139:7
Shout, "Hallelujah!"

He is wisdom.

He makes His wisdom known.
The Father reveals His secrets to us as His child, yet His wisdom is past finding out. Matt 11:25
The Son is the power and wisdom of God. 1 Cor 1:24
The Spirit is the Spirit of counsel and might. Isa 11:2

Draw near to Him.

He gives wisdom.

I speak from His counsel.
The Father gives wisdom, and from His mouth come knowledge and understanding. Pro 2:6
Jesus the Son said, "I will give you words and wisdom that none of your adversaries will be able to resist or contradict." Luke 21:15
The Spirit teaches us what to say. Luke 12:12

Recount the many blessings of His wisdom.

He is the Spirit of wisdom.

I make my boast in His truth.
The Father generously gives wisdom. James 1:5
The Son is full of grace and truth. John 1:14
The Spirit is the Spirit of wisdom and revelation, by whom I know the Father. Eph 1:17

Say, "Speak, Lord, your servant is listening."

His wisdom is a treasure.

I open my heart to His ways.
The Father's ways are unsearchable, past finding out. Rom 11:33 NKJV
The Son is unsearchable riches in whom are hidden all the treasures of wisdom and knowledge. Eph 3:8, Col 2:3
The Spirit is the Spirit of knowledge and of the fear of the Lord. Isa 11:2

Respond to His unsearchable riches of wisdom and knowledge.

He is wonder-working God.

I am in awe of His wonders.
The Father performs signs and works wonders. Exo 10:2, Ps 111:4
The Son worked miracles as Son of Man. Luke 19:37
The Spirit is the power of signs and miracles. Rom 15:19

Let everything that has breath praise the Lord.

He is the Word.

I am confident in His voice.
The Father is the word of the Lord that came to the patriarchs and prophets. Gen 15:1 (and 220 more times in the Old Testament)
The Son is the Word from the beginning (that has no beginning) and the Word of God made flesh. John 1:1,14
The Spirit speaks God's law and his Word. Zech 7:12

Thank Him that He speaks to you.

He is a man of His Word.

He is totally reliable, absolutely trustworthy, and entirely able to follow through on His Word.
The Father's words remain forever. Matt 24:35
The Son is the fulfillment of prophecy. Luke 24:44
The Spirit spoke the Scriptures long ago. Acts 1:16

Stand firm in His Word.

He is worthy of worship.

I give Him all my worship.
The Father seeks worshipers in spirit and in truth. John 4:23-24
By the Son I continually offer the sacrifice of praise to God, the fruit of my lips that confess His name. Heb 13:15
By the Spirit of God I worship and glory in Christ Jesus. Phil 3:3

Fall down and worship Him, for He is worthy.

Now it's your turn.

May this book be a giant step on your own journey deeper into the heart of God. I want this to inspire you to enrich your relationship with each person of the Trinity and to savor the richness of the Three in relationship with one another. I want you to see in all your days the weaving together of the Three like a tapestry. I pray that you will involve the Trinity in awakening in the morning and lying down to sleep at night and everything in between.

You can pray one of the following one-line prayers or declarations of faith when you feel off-kilter or when facing something important for increased strength, focus, and alignment with the purposes of God. These are powerful one-line heart cries for all of God.

I am praying for my spirit, soul, and body to stay in perfect alignment with You, Father, Son, and Holy Spirit, so that Your complete work may be accomplished in my whole being.

Take all of who I am (spirit, soul, and body) and align me with all of who You are, Father, Son, and Holy Spirit.

Father, Son, and Holy Spirit, align me with You in all of who I am, spirit, soul, and body.

Father, Son, and Holy Spirit, please give me all that I need moment by moment to be aligned with You in all I am.

I choose to align all of who I am with all of who You are, Father, Son, and Holy Spirit.

New from The Father's Business

13 week video based study for groups and individuals

Ruach Journey is an opportunity for men and women to engage with scripture in order to understand how God created us to live with our spirit, soul, and body aligned with Father, Son, and Holy Spirit. This 13 week video-based study will explore what has hindered us from living from the abundance that Jesus promised each of us as believers.

Ruach Journey includes practical ways to bless and nourish our spirits and also how to recognize when we are living in less than God designed. Ruach Journey is an invitation to discover the richness of the treasure He has placed in you—spirit, soul, and body. In this study, Sylvia Gunter and Elizabeth Gunter will take you deeper into the themes and concepts of You Are Blessed In The Names of God and Free To Be You.

Resources Available

Ruach Journey Study Guide—13 weeks of interactive study including listening guides, discussion questions, and between session activities.

Leader's Kit—Contains one Study Guide, one Leader's Guide, Free To Be You, and a set of 8 DVDs.

Order at www.thefathersbusiness.com

More Books From The Father's Business

All resources are available at www.thefathersbusiness.com

Blessing For Life: Words Of Hope and Healing
What may seem like a few simple words can bring hope and healing to very dry ground in yourself and others. That is what blessing the spirit is all about. This book contains a short teaching on the biblical foundation for blessing your spirit and 50 blessings for all of life.

For The Family
48 pages of powerful prayers for husbands and wives, moms and dads, who want to pray God's heart and see Him glorified in your family. It is intended for those who need a starting point for intercession for your family and those who need fresh weapons in the battle.

Safe In The Father's Heart
This is an invitation to wholeness, peace, and joy as you live in God's delight in you as His child. This book is Sylvia's story of discovering and experiencing the Father heart of God. God is powerful enough to create the universe and personal enough to delight in holding you in His Father heart.

Study Guide for Safe In The Father's Heart
10-week study guide for use by individuals and groups goes deeper into the principles in Safe In The Father's Heart.

You Are Blessed In The Names Of God
with 112 blessings and 32 pages of teaching.
God meets His children at their place of need through blessings. These blessings are designed to draw you closer to Him, aligning your spirit with His spirit in His perfect love.